The ADMIRAL'S ACADEMY

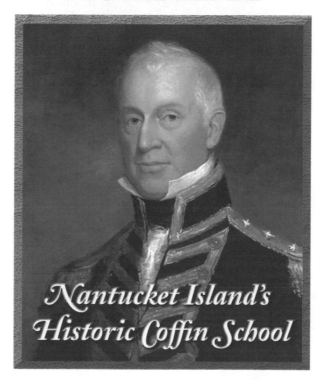

Nantucket Island's Historic Coffin School

MARGARET MOORE BOOKER

MILL HILL PRESS   NANTUCKET, MASSACHUSETTS

Mill Hill Press was established to preserve and record
the history of Nantucket Island and the people who live
by the sea–for therein lies, in great part, the story of America.

Hope you enjoy this offering from Mill Hill.

Albert F. Egan

Albert F. Egan, Jr., Publisher
Mill Hill Press

MILL HILL PRESS
134 ORANGE STREET
NANTUCKET, MASSACHUSETTS 02554

LIBRARY OF CONGRESS CATALOG CARD NUMBER: 98-066191
ISBN 0-9638910-9-x

MANUFACTURED IN THE UNITED STATES OF AMERICA

FOR MARTY

This engraving of the historic Coffin School on Nantucket Island was reproduced in *Scribner's Monthly*, August 1873. Built in 1852–54, the Greek Revival style brick building is a monument to the founder of the school, Admiral Sir Isaac Coffin, and serves as a unique expression of the island's history.

Contents

ILLUSTRATIONS

ACKNOWLEDGMENTS

Special thanks to Albert F. Egan, Jr., for giving me the opportunity to write this book; Nathaniel Philbrick, director of the Egan Institute of Maritime Studies, for his encouragement, guidance, and sharing of research material; Jean Hughes and the Coffin School Trustees, for their support and unlimited access to the school archives; Peter Gow, for his patience and expert editing skills; Elizabeth Oldham, for her superb copyediting; and Coffin School alumni, for sharing their memories with me, especially Jane Richmond, Ruth Grieder, David D. Worth, and all those who participated in the October 1996 gam.

For their generous research assistance, many thanks to the staffs of the following organizations: the Nantucket Historical Association, especially Aimee Newell, Betsy Lowenstein, Mary Woodruff, Michael Jehle, and Peter MacGlashan; the Nantucket Atheneum, especially Sharon Carlee, and Betsy Tyler; and the Boston Athenaeum, including Michael Wentworth and Catharina Slautterback.

Finally, a heartfelt thanks to my husband, Martin Booker, and my family, for their kind and loving encouragement and support.

I

ADMIRAL SIR ISAAC COFFIN

"Great Admiral, while tides shall flow
Around Nantucket's grateful shore,
The gift you gave shall larger grow,
Your name be blest forevermore."

W. Frederick Brown,
Inquirer and Mirror, 1906

A stately presence on Winter Street in Nantucket town, the Coffin School stands as a unique expression of the island's history. While the brickwork pediment and simple fluted white columns proclaim the democratic virtues of the young United States, the building's heritage is curiously aristocratic. Rather than an early settler, it is a British admiral, a titled hero of the Revolutionary War, who gave his name– and a considerable part of his fortune–to establish the school as a memorial to his family's role in island history.

Boston-born and bred, Admiral Sir Isaac Coffin enjoyed a successful forty-year career in the Royal Navy. Although he fought on the side of the British during the American Revolution, he never lost his love and deep admiration for what he called "my native land," crossing the Atlantic more than thirty times during his lifetime.[1] In his desire to support his American kin, he sent English racehorses to improve the American breed, imported rare fruits and plants for American horticulturists, and brought the first European turbot to New England waters.

The admiral's most notable philanthropic gesture was the founding of a Lancasterian school on Nantucket Island. A fifth-generation descendant of Tristram Coffin—one of the first English settlers on Nantucket in 1660—Sir Isaac was particularly proud of his island heritage. The fact that the Coffins had helped to build the foremost whaling port in the world must have appealed to the admiral's nautical and American interests.

Born in Boston in 1759, Isaac Coffin was the youngest son of Nathaniel, cashier of the port's Customs House, and Elizabeth (Barnes) Coffin. When he was eight years old, he was sent to the Boston Latin School, where he excelled in science and nautical studies. A boisterous boy, he led the sports activities at school, and as the champion of the "Southender" boys, he was often in "frequent battles with foot- or snowball, or with fisticuffs."[2] Isaac's family was inclined to what would be termed loyalist views in the coming Revolution, and, in 1773, he entered the Royal Navy as a midshipman on the *Gaspé*; by July 1778, with war raging between his native colonies and the British government, he was appointed lieutenant. He served on various ships during the Revolution and was a signal officer aboard the *Royal Oak* during a decisive battle with the French. Isaac's success in gaining promotions in the Royal Navy may have been partly a result of his connections with the royal family. According to an early nineteenth-century account of Isaac's career, he had, throughout his life, the "favour and approbation of his adopted sovereign" and in his youth had been a sailing companion of William the Fourth, later known as the "Sailor King."[3]

By age twenty-two, Coffin was promoted to commander and sailed with Admiral Alexander Hood in the Battle of the Saints during Britain's campaign against the French in the West Indies. His return to England was marred by a court martial brought against him for the common charge of signing a false muster. Instead of bothering with the bureaucratic red tape required for reinstatement, Coffin quit the navy to join the patriots of Brabant fighting for independence from Austria.[4] When the Admiralty realized it might lose one of its finest officers, Coffin was honorably acquitted. He was then reinstated, and in 1790 he was appointed to the 28-gun frigate *Alligator*. While his ship was lying in Nore, one of Coffin's men fell overboard in a gale, and Coffin dove in after him. Although he saved the sailor, he suffered an abdominal injury that would plague him for the rest of his life.

Coffin charted the St. Lawrence River and served as commissioner of the British Navy at Corsica, Lisbon, Minorca, Halifax, and Sheerness. Due to poor health, he was unable to undertake active duty, but he did gain a reputation as an energetic and efficient commissioner. As a result of his efforts, on April 23, 1804, he was appointed rear admiral of the White Squadron, placing him in the top echelon of the Royal Navy's seaborne commanders. One month later, "as a farther mark of his Sovereign's favour, and for his unremitting zeal and persevering efforts for the good of his Majesty's Navy," Admiral Coffin was made a Baronet of the United Kingdom of Great Britain and Ireland.[5] The admiral served as superintendent at Portsmouth until he was promoted to vice admiral in 1808, and subsequently retired.

According to one account, Sir Isaac Coffin had a "jovial nature" that was "contagious and irresistible." But not everyone approved of his lively nature. In 1811, the admiral married Elizabeth Browne Greenly, the only daughter of William Greenly of Herefordshire. Her family did not appreciate the admiral's "hearty and jovial" ways and the match proved unsuccessful. According to one early biographer, the couple did not get along, because the aristocratic Lady Elizabeth "was said to be addicted to writing sermons at night, to the disturbance of the slumbers of her rollicking spouse, and so, after a space they separated."[6] Although the admiral had assumed the name and arms of Greenly, he dropped them in 1813. The couple separated amicably and continued to correspond regularly.

Admiral Coffin also corresponded with the infamous Lady Hamilton, whom he visited in the 1790s at her mansion in Naples, and with his good friend Lord Nelson–the most renowned naval commander of his age.

On 14 June 1814, Coffin was appointed a full admiral, and from 1818 to 1826 he served as a member of the British Parliament for the borough of Ilchester. By this date the admiral–who was illustrious enough to have been painted by both Gilbert Stuart and court painter Sir William Beechey–had accumulated a sizable estate from well-invested naval pay and prize money from his naval victories. Also, in recognition of his public service, the Magdalen Islands, at the mouth of the St. Lawrence River, had been granted to the admiral by order of King George III in 1798.

The Founding of an Academy

In September 1826, at the age of sixty-seven, the admiral left his home in England to visit his Coffin relatives on Nantucket Island.[7] The local paper reported that he felt immediately at home: "During his stay upon the island, he visited our principle places of resort, discarding the rules of court etiquette, and mingling freely with the republican populace."[8]

The admiral's visit to Nantucket was commemorated by a bronze medal he had struck for that occasion, bearing a likeness of Tristram

Coffin and the date 1642, the year the Coffin family first arrived in the New World.[9] Encircling the image is the inscription: "Tristram Coffin, the first of the race that settled in America." On the obverse are four hands joined together surrounded with the injunction "Do honor to his name–be united."

During his visit the admiral stayed with William Coffin, an influential merchant, in his home at 18 Union Street. Here he met the latter's son-in-law, Samuel Haynes Jenks, then editor of the *Inquirer*. For several years, Jenks had been trying to persuade the town of Nantucket to establish a system of public schools on the island. The admiral, who had no one to inherit his considerable estate, asked Jenks what memorial he could leave that would benefit his island kin and perpetuate his name. The following is an account of the occasion and Jenks's reply:

> I took the gouty old hero in a chaise to Siasconset. On the way he disclosed to me the object of his visit. It was, he said, having no immediate heirs, to "do something to cause his name to be remembered." "Should he build a church," he asked, "or raise a great monument, or purchase a ship for the town's benefit?" Full of the enthusiasm and zeal with which I had so long been excited on the subject of schools, a thought at once struck me. "If you raise a monument, Sir Isaac, I said, it will not be looked at by more than a hundred people once a year; if you build a church, as you are an Episcopalian, it will neither be supported nor attended, for there is scarcely one besides myself of that order in the place; and as to the purchase of a vessel, if done at all, it should be for purposes of nautical instruction. The best thing you can do–the deed that will make you forever remembered–is to establish and endow a free school…You will thus benefit your numerous kinsfolk and their grateful posterity, while you effectually perpetuate your name." [10]

The Admiral immediately set out to bring Jenks's ideas to fruition. He authorized William Coffin to purchase a building on the corner of Fair and Lyon streets that had formerly been a Nantucket Lancasterian school established by the Methodist Society. The schoolhouse was purchased on September 9, 1826, for $1,300. An additional $100 was spent on fitting out the building. Many supplies were purchased for the school at an auction, including an "excellent bell" weighing one hundred pounds.[11]

One of the admiral's hopes was that the new school would give Nantucket children the same quality of education he had received in Boston, to which he often attributed his own success in life. From Charleston, South Carolina, on March 20, 1827, he wrote to William Coffin that a board should be neatly painted with his name as founder of the school and placed in a conspicuous spot on the new building, so "that the rising Generation should know that by Morality, Exertion, Enterprize & Probity, they have a chance of attaining the same Honor, Happiness, & Prosperity, which their Relation the Founder of the School has done." [12]

An act of incorporation was passed by the Massachusetts legislature on 8 June 1827, establishing the Admiral Sir Isaac Coffin's Lancasterian School, "for the purpose of promoting decency, good order and morality, and for giving a good English education to youth who are descendants of the late Tristram Coffin...." At that time a majority of the island's population of more than 8,000 people could trace their roots to Tristram. The charter placed the school in the control of a board of trustees who were appointed by the admiral. As the first president and treasurer of the board, he selected the man who had first introduced him to the island, William Coffin. The other board members were Ariel Coffin, Gorham Coffin, Jared Coffin, Captain Thaddeus Coffin, and whale oil merchant Charles G. Coffin. A proviso was made that all the trustees should be descendants of Tristram Coffin.

In 1827, the admiral gave $100 to the trustees for books and other supplies and that same year set up an endowment of £2500 for the school. This was heralded by the *Boston Globe* as the largest gift ever devoted to a public purpose in the Commonwealth by a private person.[13] In 1835, the admiral gave an additional £3333, with the income to be used for buying books for the library and other general expenses.

At the time the Coffin School was founded, there were no public schools on the island, primarily because the island's influential Quaker community (which maintained its own schools) had long been reluctant to contribute financially to the education of non-Quakers.[14] As a consequence, it was estimated that more than three hundred Nantucket children were without the benefit of any formal education. Prompted in part by the admiral's decision to open a school, the town, in May of 1827, finally appropriated the sum of two thousand dollars to establish public schools on the island. An article on the founding of the school claimed that the "town itself, provoked and ashamed, as it were, by this magnanimous example, was incited to the erection of three similar schools."[15]

Fig. 1 *Sir Isaac Coffin, Bart.*, engraving by William Ridley after an original miniature, published by I. Gold, Shoe Lane, London, August 1, 1804. Based on an earlier portrait, this likeness was engraved and printed at the height of the admiral's career in the British navy, just a few months after he had been appointed rear admiral of the White Squadron and been made a baronet. *Collection of the Coffin School Trustees.*

Fig. 2 Sir William Beechey, *Admiral Sir Isaac Coffin*, 1808, oil on canvas. Painted in London, this likeness confirms Thomas Amory's description of the admiral as being "tall, robust, but of symmetrical proportions…and his countenance expressive and noble." The portrait was purchased for the school in 1847, for $50, from Mrs. Hector Coffin in Lynn, Massachusetts, to replace the 1810 portrait of the Admiral by Gilbert Stuart that had been burned in the Great Fire of 1846. It hung in the Atheneum until the new schoolhouse was built on Winter Street in 1852–54. Sir William Beechey (1753–1839) studied at the Royal Academy and became known for his accurate renderings of the royal family and other distinguished members of British society. *Photo by Terry Pommett. Collection of the Coffin School Trustees.*

Fig. 3   Denis Dighton, *Admiral Sir Isaac Coffin*, 1809, watercolor and gouache on paper. Shown here in the full dress of an admiral, Sir Isaac Coffin had by the date this portrait was painted retired from active naval service. The background harbor scene depicted in this work has not been identified. Dighton studied and exhibited at the Royal Academy. He served in the British Army 1801–1815 and was a military draftsman to the Prince of Wales. *Collection of the Coffin School Trustees.*

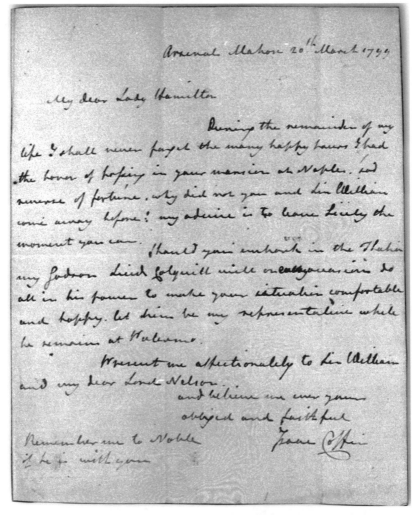

Fig. 4 *Letter from Admiral Coffin to Lady Emma Hamilton, March 20, 1799.* Among the famous people with whom Admiral Coffin corresponded was Lady Hamilton, famed paramour of Lord Nelson. In this letter the admiral gives a tantalizing hint of his close relationship with the lady: "During the remainder of my life I shall never forget the many happy hours I had the honor of passing in your mansion at Naples." *Photo by Terry Pommett. Courtesy of the Nantucket Historical Association.*

Fig. 5 William Behnes, *Admiral Sir Isaac Coffin*, 1826, marble. A London artist who specialized in portrait busts, William Behnes made this sculpture of the admiral, who gave it to the Boston Athenaeum in 1827. Two plaster copies of the bust were given to the Coffin School and placed in the first schoolhouse on Fair Street. *Courtesy of the Boston Athenaeum.*

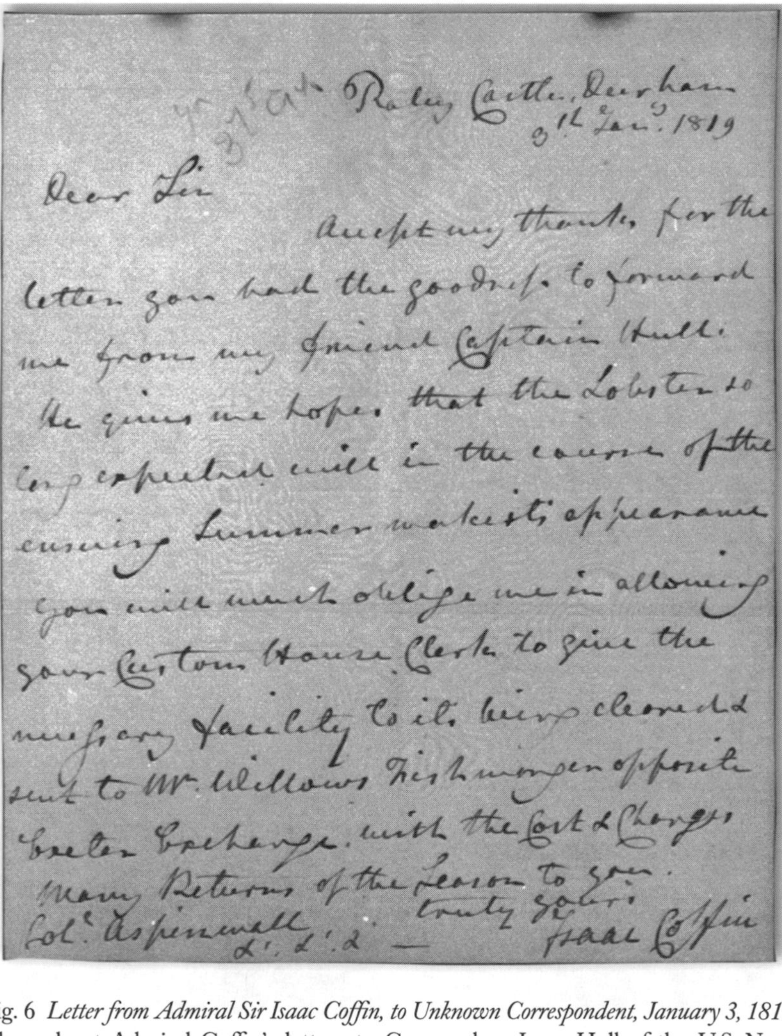

Raby Castle, Durham
3rd Jan.y 1819

Dear Sir

Accept my thanks for the
letter you had the goodness to forward
me from my friend Captain Hull.
He gives me hopes that the Lobster so
long expected will in the course of the
ensuing summer make its appearance
You will much oblige me in allowing
your Custom House Clerk to give the
necessary facility to its being cleared &
sent to Mr. Willows Fishmonger opposite
Exeter Exchange, with the Cost & Charges.
Many Returns of the Season to you.
truly Yours
Col.l Aspinwall
£1.1.2 —
Isaac Coffin

Fig. 6 *Letter from Admiral Sir Isaac Coffin, to Unknown Correspondent, January 3, 1819.* Throughout Admiral Coffin's letters to Commodore Isaac Hull of the U.S. Navy (renowned commander of the USS *Constitution* in the War of 1812) are repeated requests that Hull send him the largest Boston lobster he can find. Here, the admiral writes that a letter from his "friend Captain Hull" gives him hope "that the Lobster so long expected will in the course of the ensuing summer make its appearance." *Photo by Terry Pommett. Courtesy of the Nantucket Historical Association.*

Fig. 7 Samuel Stillman Osgood, *Admiral Sir Isaac Coffin*, 1830, oil on canvas. The admiral met Osgood in 1830, when they were both stranded in the same lifeboat after the ship they were traveling in was struck by lightning and burned. Osgood painted the admiral's portrait after they returned safely to Boston. Coffin donated the work "by a fellow sufferer" to the Boston Athenaeum in 1830. *Courtesy of the Boston Athenaeum.*

Fig. 8 Dominic W. Boudet, *Samuel Haynes Jenks*, 1839, oil on canvas. Editor of the Nantucket *Inquirer,* Jenks had encouraged Admiral Sir Isaac Coffin, during his trip to the island in 1826, to found a school as a memorial and to benefit the Admiral's island kin. Jenks eventually enrolled his own children in the Coffin School. Boudet was an itinerant portrait miniature and history painter active ca. 1805–45. *Courtesy of the Nantucket Historical Association.*

Fig. 9 Attributed to William Swain, *The Honorable William Coffin*, ca. 1830, oil on canvas. William Coffin was an influential merchant on Nantucket and was appointed by Admiral Sir Isaac Coffin as the first president of the Coffin School trustees. The portrait was given to the trustees in 1904 by Maria L. Owen, who attended the Coffin School and was William Coffin's granddaughter. The work has been attributed to William Swain–Nantucket's foremost portraitist in the 1820s and 1830s – but definitive proof of this authorship has not yet been discovered. *Photo by Terry Pommett. Collection of the Coffin School Trustees.*

Fig. 10 William Swain, *Charles G. Coffin,* ca. 1830, oil on canvas. The son of Zenas Coffin and brother of Henry G. Coffin, Charles G. Coffin was a successful whaling merchant on Nantucket. He was appointed by Admiral Sir Isaac Coffin as one of the first trustees of the Coffin School in 1827, and when he died in 1882, at the age of eighty, he was the last original trustee serving on the board. The portrait was given to the school in 1915 by Mary C. Green, Charles Coffin's daughter. *Photo by Terry Pommett. Collection of the Coffin School Trustees.*

Fig. 11   *Facsimile of Tristram Coffin Medal,* 1881. To commemorate his visit to Nantucket in 1826, Admiral Coffin had bronze medals struck bearing a likeness of Tristram Coffin and the date 1642, the year the Coffin family settled in America. He later distributed one medal to each of the Coffin School trustees. *Photo by Terry Pommett. Courtesy of the Nantucket Historical Association.*

2

The Early Years: 1827–1846

In the spring of 1827, Admiral Sir Isaac Coffin's Lancasterian School opened in the Fair Street building, with the boys department commencing May 1, and the girls department June 1. The first class totaled two hundred and thirty scholars, ranging in age from seven to sixteen. William Coffin, Jr., son of the president of the school's board, was the first "preceptor" of the boys, with an annual salary of five hundred dollars plus seventy-five cents per scholar; and Almira Meach was "preceptress" of the girls, receiving three hundred dollars per year plus one dollar for each student over one hundred in her department.[1] Educated at Harvard University, William Coffin, Jr., who also served as principal of the school, was said to have an "enthusiastic love of literature" and an "ardent attachment to the interests of education."[2]

Separated by gender in two rooms, each containing a plaster bust of the admiral, the scholars pursued the same studies and recited together.[3] Depending on the student's level, he or she took courses in the following subjects: reading, writing, spelling, arithmetic, geometry, algebra, declamation, rhetoric, chemistry, grammar, history, and natural philosophy. In addition, one day a week the girls were taught needlework by Almira Meach, and, in 1829, a course in penmanship was offered by a Captain William Noyes for the female department. Later, French, linear drawing, astronomy, and bookkeeping were added to the curriculum.

Beginning in November of 1827, a public exhibition featuring student plays, recitations, and musical performances was held once a year on a stage erected specifically for the purpose. According to William Coffin, the first "performance astonished the audience, which was large say [–] five or six hundred including all the Parents of the children...."[4]

School examinations were held quarterly and vacations were scheduled by the teachers, except for one fixed week during the sheep-shearing season in June.

Initially, classes were taught under the then-popular Lancasterian method. Established in England in the 1790s by Joseph Lancaster, the system involved using the brightest students as monitors and tutors, with one class teaching what it had learned to the class below. Since it minimized the number of teachers required, one of the attractions of the Lancasterian system was its relatively low cost. It also included a reward system–giving out medals or some other token–that put students of the same ability in competition with each other. In December 1827, the admiral sent a box of medals to the school from England, and instructed the trustees: "Six to be delivered annually to the most deserving of each Sex. In time we may be able to give Silver ones."[5]

Early record books survive that give us a glimpse into school life.

There are lists of students who were awarded medals and tokens for excelling in their studies, as well as lists of students with demerits. Each scholar's daily conduct was carefully recorded; in 1836, a teacher noted that Thomas B. Swain was "truent [*sic*], as usual" and in 1837, a teacher wrote: "The scholars are seated in such a manner that the most roguish are at a distance from each other."[6] A list of scholars who attended the school from 1837 through 1839 records that Charlie D. Pinkham entered school in 1838 but was later "lost at sea."[7]

Although the admiral intended that the school be open to all Coffin descendants, he insisted on charging a small tuition, telling Samuel Jenks: "Egad, what costs nothing is never valued."[8] In addition, by many accounts, it was apparent that the endowment set up by the admiral was not sufficient to support the school. The tuition began at fifty cents per quarter, not including costs of books and stationery. By the early 1830s, it was two dollars and fifty cents per term. Those who could not trace their genealogy back to Tristram Coffin, the "patriarch of 1640," could attend the school, but had to pay fifty cents more per quarter.[9]

Most accounts of the school's opening were positive. A report on the new public schools in the *Inquirer* of 7 September 1827 noted that "We also visited the Coffin School and heard the children go through some of their exercises, with which we were pleased. This instruction [promises] to become of vast importance to this community." However, one early reference, written by the island's first historian, Obed Macy, expresses reservations on the part of some islanders about sending their children to an institution funded by a British admiral: "A very great change has of late taken place among us, respecting the school education of the children. Admiral Isaac Coffin of the British Navy from motives of benevolence towards all the decendants of Tristram Coffin.... & probably from a desire of popular applause of the people of this island, has established a fund for the establishment & support of a school for all the descendants of the aforesaid Tristram Coffin…. The school at present appears likely to succeed to expectations. Some appear rather scrupulous in partaking of the benefit of the institution, established by money obtained in the British Navy." [10]

The admiral's vision for the school included nautical training for the boys. In 1828, he wrote to William Coffin, "As to the Boys, I wish them to have an education suitable to the Line of Life they are likely to move in and as many of them will go to sea a good knowledge of mathematics to be instilled into their minds before they start." [11]

To fully educate Nantucket boys in navigation and other nautical skills, the admiral purchased the brig *Clio* for the school in 1829 and had it specially equipped for educational purposes. [12] Built in Barnstable in 1822, the ship was 179 tons and eighty-seven feet long. Although it was to be short-lived, the admiral's "floating school" was the first training ship in America. On the *Clio*, commanded by Lieutenant Alexander Pinkham, on leave from the United States Navy after sixteen years of service, Nantucket boys studied navigation, astronomy, joining, carpentry, blacksmithing, and other subjects as well as practical seamanship.

In his instructions for the *Clio*, the admiral dictated what the sailors would wear: "…blue jackets and trousers of good cloth, blue knit stockings (of worsted in winter and cotton in summer). On the right arm…a red anchor…great coats…lined with baize made of No. 6 canvas and painted." [13] He also insisted that before the boys set off on a voyage, they should be provided with "plenty of pumpkins, squashes, apples and good advice." [14]

Unfortunately, the *Clio* venture was to be a stormy one. Twenty-one Coffin School boys, ranging in age from twelve to sixteen, and a small amount of freight to help defray the cost of the voyage, set out for Boston in August 1829. While moored in Boston harbor, a banquet was held on the quarterdeck, presided over by the admiral and attended by city officials. On September ninth, the brig left the harbor and over the next few months visited the ports of Quebec, the Magdalen Islands, and Pictou, Nova Scotia. One of the boys, Andrew J. Morton, later recalled: "It was a cold voyage for boys of 13 years of age, I tell you."[15] When the brig returned to Boston in November, nine boys returned home without permission from the captain, one was dismissed, and two more were discharged at their parents' request. On December 22, 1829, with only eight Coffin School boys, the brig sailed for the port of Rio Grande on the coast of Brazil.

In May of 1830, Captain Pinkham wrote a detailed account of the brig's trip to Brazil for the school's trustees, in response to what he termed "slanderous" reports of his treatment of the boys. Pinkham himself admitted that if a boy broke the rules, he was "immediately set to work scraping the deck."[16] Among the topics he describes are the logbooks kept by the boys, rowing and sailing matches, students learning to rig sails, boys getting stomachaches from gorging themselves on oranges, and even the purchase of an artificial flower arrangement for the Coffin School preceptress, Almira Meach. The admiral defended Captain Pinkham's actions in a letter he wrote from Charleston on 19 January 1830.

The *Clio* proved to be an unprofitable concern, and further trouble arose on the Quebec voyage when the Canadians expressed their extreme displeasure that a British admiral was funding the nautical training of a rival nation. The trustees of the Coffin School sold the *Clio* in 1831, thus abruptly ending the first schoolship program in the United States.

Partly as a result of the criticism that reached England over the Quebec incident, Admiral Coffin lost his chance of being appointed the new Earl of Magdalen, even though he had been nominated for the post by his good friend William the Fourth, the "Sailor King."

In late July and early August 1829, the admiral braved the high seas to visit Nantucket for a second (or perhaps third) time. The local paper reported that upon his arrival a large crowd of people gathered on the wharf "to welcome their distinguished friend and benefactor with cheers and other demonstrations of joy." [17] On the afternoon of that same day, after a short rest in the mansion of Jared Coffin (one of the Coffin School trustees), the admiral was greeted by a procession of students led by preceptor Coffin and preceptress Meach. They accompanied the admiral to the schoolhouse, where an address was given by Andrew M. Macy, aged 14, followed by a poem written by Sarah C. Bunker, aged 15, which was recited in unison by all the students:

> Again thy safe return we greet,
> Our hearts with joy and rapture beat,
> Our benefactor thus to meet,
> A welcome guest;
> While gratitude with transport sweet
> Inspires each breast.
>
> Encircled with a wreath of Fame,
> Perpetual honors crown thy name,
> Thy generous bounty we'll proclaim,
> With hearts sincere;
> And while we may thy kindred claim,
> Thy name revere. [18]

According to the newspaper, the admiral was overwhelmed by the ceremony:

> When he addressed the school, the organs of speech were inadequate to give utterance to the feelings of his heart–the tears that trickled down his venerable cheeks were the purest that benevolence could give, and the most undeceiving token of the sublime satisfaction which dilated his glowing breast, when witnessing a scene so delightful as that of several hundred scholars, happy in the pursuit of

science under his munificence. On this occasion, the gallant
spirit of the brave Admiral was softened into tears, but they
were tears of gladness.[19]

In the days following the presentation, the admiral visited the school
to observe classes during routine exercises. He spoke to the students,
expressing "his entire satisfaction with the progress of improvement in
the various branches of learning taught in the school." At the time of his
visit, there were close to two hundred and fifty students, although the
number would gradually diminish as the new public schools became
increasingly popular. When the admiral left the island for Boston
accompanied by William Coffin, the newspaper reported that the
"benediction of thousands accompanied his departure."[20]

During the last ten years of his life, Admiral Coffin continued to
correspond with the trustees and show interest in every aspect of the
school. William Coffin, president of the trustees, wrote to him of the
school's progress and successful improvement of the scholars at
examination time. As time went on, the admiral increasingly deferred
to the trustees' judgment. At age seventy-two, he wrote from London,
on 1 January 1832, "Your last Dispatch...has gratified me exceedingly,
nothing being nearer my Heart than the great Improvement of the
School bearing my Name & instituted for the Benefit of my Poor
Relations.... [W]hen next you visit the School please to remember me
kindly to the rising Generation & offer my best wishes to all relations
& friends in the Island."[21] In April of 1834, he wrote from London that
he was transferring £3333 to the mayor of Boston for the trustees of
the school, with the stipulation that during the first ten years dividends
from the funds be used to purchase books to form a library for the
school. After ten years, the dividends were to be given to five boys and
five girls recommended by the trustees.

The admiral's health continued to decline. On 24 June 1835, he wrote
"My Infirmities Gout & Rheumatism have so increased as to Deprive me
of the use of my Legs, still my Spirits are as good as ever, though I have

passed my seventy sixth year. I have withdrawn from public Life altogether…. "[22] Four years later he died in Cheltenham, England.

By 1831, the Coffin School had dispensed with the Lancasterian, or monitorial plan. In his *History of Nantucket*, published in 1835, Obed Macy described the new plan: "The pupils are now arranged in four classes…. The fourth, or primary class, is preparatory to the third, and studies are laid out for the three higher classes, calculated to occupy each class one year. Class succeeds class precisely on the college plan. Those who have attended the school three whole years, and completed the studies of the first class, are entitled to one year's tuition gratis…." An advertisement in the *Inquirer* also described the new plan, listing the courses each class would take.[23] As previously, the girls and boys were taught separately but gave their recitations together. William Coffin, Jr., was still principal of the male department, with Andrew M. Macy as his assistant, and Lydia Barney was the principal of the female department, with Susan Easton as her assistant. Tuition was $2.50 per term.

After the new plan had been in place for five years, trustee Gorham Coffin assured the admiral that although the number of students had declined, the school's original purposes were still being fulfilled:

> The School continues to maintain its character…. The average number of Scholars is about fifty male and sixty female: price of tuition two & a half dollars per quarter to those who are able to pay; some are admitted at a less price & some are admitted gratis. The male department is under the care of Mr. Luther Robinson, a graduate of Brown University, at a salary of $700. per Annum: He is a very amiable young man, well qualified to fill the station…. The female department continues under the care of Miss Lydia Barney, at a Salary of $300. per Annum: She is a teacher of the first order, of her sex. Each department of the School has an assistant at a salary of $100 per Annum."[24]

Attesting to the high quality of instruction at the Coffin School is that many of the early students went on to become teachers, while others made names for themselves in other professions. For instance, Roland H. Macy attended the school in 1831–33 and founded Macy's department store in New York City in 1858; George G. Fish attended the school in 1839 and became a well-known artist on the island.

As a result of the anti-Masonic movement sweeping the country in the first half of the nineteenth century, the island's Masonic Association, Union Lodge No. 5, transferred its building and land on Main Street to the trustees of the Coffin School in 1836. Under the agreement the school would receive one fourth of the interest from the funds to purchase scientific equipment for the school. The Coffin School trustees were to pay the lodge the remaining three-fourths of the interest from the funds. One of the stipulations was that the school admit "children, whether of the Coffin family or not, as may be designated for that purpose by the Master and Wardens of the Lodge upon the same terms and under the same regulations as those of the Coffin Family are received."[25]

Also, as it was thought at that time that the Freemasons would likely disband, an agreement was made that if the lodge ever ceased to exist, the fund would become the property of the school. In 1838 the lodge building and land were sold to William Coffin for $2,500 and the trustees invested the proceeds in securities. In the early 1900s, the fund was yielding the school about two hundred dollars a year. Not until 1921 did the trustees of the school and the trustees of the Union Lodge decide to divide the principal of what was called "the Masonic Fund"–three-quarters to the Masons and one quarter to the school.

By the 1830s, the Coffin School had created a library situated on the third floor of a building at the corner of Main and Centre streets that was owned and occupied by the Nantucket Institution for Savings. Students were charged seven cents quarterly for the use of the library (which contained as many as 3,000 volumes) and were allowed to take out one book at a time for a period of one week.[26] On the night of 13 July 1846, a fire broke out on the south side of Main Street, destroying two-thirds of the town, including the building housing the library. In addition to the books, a portrait of Admiral Coffin painted by Gilbert Stuart and a plaster bust of the admiral made from the marble original in the Boston Athenaeum were lost.[27] As one later source stated, the destruction of the Atheneum library and "the loss at the same time of that of the Coffin School and many private libraries, left the inhabitants of the island more destitute of reading resources than ever before."[28]

As a result of the fire and the decline in the island's whaling industry, the Coffin School was forced to close its doors in 1846. The trustees thought it was best to allow time for the endowment fund to accumulate. Two years later, the building and land on Fair Street were sold.

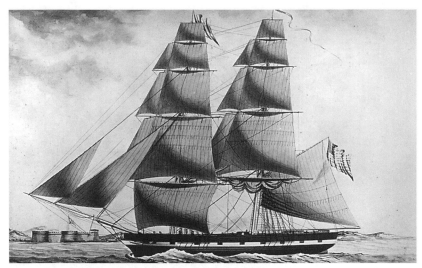

Fig. 12 E. Camillati, *The Brig* Leander *of Salem*, 1830, watercolor on paper. The brig *Leander*, built in Salem in 1821, was of the same vintage and general style as the Coffin School's "floating school," the brig *Clio*, for which no representation can be found. Built in Barnstable in 1822, the *Clio* was a hundred and seventy-nine tons and eighty-seven feet long. *Courtesy of the Peabody Essex Museum, Salem, Massachusetts.*

Fig. 13 William Swain, *Lieutenant Alexander Pinkham*, 1830, oil on canvas. Born in Nantucket, Alexander Pinkham served in the United States Navy for sixteen years before taking command of the *Clio*. It may have been due to his strictness with the boys that many of them abruptly cut short their participation in the program and returned home before the second voyage. The portrait was given to the Coffin School in 1901 by his niece, Mrs. Harriet G. Calder. *Courtesy of the Nantucket Historical Association.*

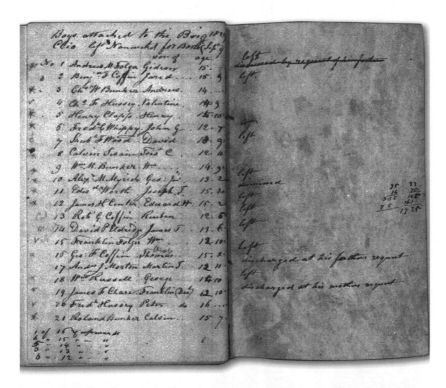

Fig. 14 *List of Students on the* Clio, 1829. In August 1829, twenty-one Coffin School boys set off on the *Clio*. After trips to Quebec, the Magdalen Islands, and Nova Scotia, the brig returned to Boston. Before it took off again for Brazil, thirteen of the boys returned home to Nantucket rather than continue on. Note the additions to this list on the right-hand side, indicating that many of the boys left without permission or were discharged by their parents. *Photo by Terry Pommett. Courtesy of the Nantucket Historical Association.*

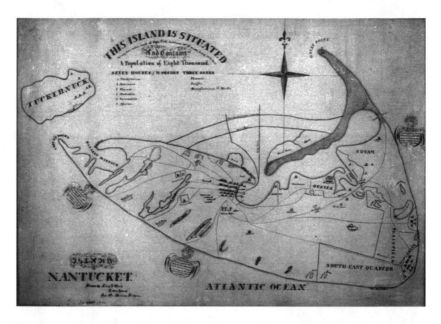

Fig. 15 Lucy S. Macy, *Map of Nantucket*, ca. 1829, watercolor and ink on paper. Born on Nantucket in 1812, Lucy Swain Macy was a student at the Coffin School in 1828–29, during which time she drew this intricate map of the island. She was awarded two medals for her work at the school, one of which may have been for this map. *Photo by Terry Pommett. Courtesy of the Nantucket Historical Association.*

Fig. 16 James S. Hathaway, *Augustus Morse*, ca. 1845, oil on canvas. Morse attended Dartmouth College and after fourteen years of service in Vermont schools, he came to Nantucket in 1837 to become a teacher at the Coffin School on Fair Street. His assistant was Rebecca Clapp, whom he married in 1839. That same year he was appointed principal of the Nantucket High School, a position he held for sixteen years. Hathaway was a portraitist active on Nantucket in the 1840s. *Courtesy of the Nantucket Historical Association.*

3

A New Greek Revival Home: 1854–1898

On 28 January 1846, Charles G. Coffin had sold to the Coffin School trustees land and a building on Winter Street for $1,600. In 1852–54, an impressive new schoolhouse was built on the land, paid for by the income–between eight and nine thousand dollars–from the endowment that had accumulated during the years the school was closed. A committee of four trustees led by Charles G. Coffin and Robert M. Joy was appointed to superintend the construction of a brick Greek Revival-style building, with marble steps leading up to a recessed portico, flanked by two white Doric columns of wood.

On the marble lintel of the portico, facing all who entered the building, were inscribed the words "Founded 1827, By Admiral Sir Isaac Coffin, Bart." in keeping with the admiral's original request that a sign be erected in a conspicuous place outside the schoolhouse indicating that he was the founder. The schoolyard was enclosed by an elaborate wrought-iron fence. Over the decades, the fence seems to have been a great temptation to mischief makers, who on two occasions had the audacity to tear down and break a portion of it.[1]

Although no architect of the schoolhouse is known, an early record book indicates that the firm of James Thompson and Edward Easton were the primary builders.[2] In planning the school, they may have consulted books of architectural plans and drawings, through whose popularity the Greek Revival style–seen as a visual statement of democratic principles–spread across the nation.

When the building opened in September 1854, the trustees continued to charge tuition and organized the school as an academy, offering the "common branches" of study, "classical studies," and college-preparatory courses. Classes were held six days a week. New to the curriculum were Latin, French, German, and music. The academy flourished under principal Alfred Macy, Esq., who served through the spring of 1861. He was assisted by Anne Mitchell, who taught languages, and Philinda D. Fisher and Helen M. Pinkham. Anne was the daughter of William and Lydia Mitchell of Nantucket and the sister of famed astronomer Maria Mitchell. Known around town as a master of languages, she taught at the Coffin School until she married Alfred Macy in 1857.[3] When Fisher resigned in 1858, her replacement was Susan H. Coleman, whom Alfred Macy later described as one of the best teachers "on the face of the Globe."[4]

After Alfred Macy left his position to practice law, he was replaced by Nantucket grammar school teacher Seymour L. Meade, from 1861 to 1867, with Susan Coleman as his first assistant. Meade was followed by F.B. Mildram, from 1867 to 1869, with Helen Gardner as first assistant.

In 1854, Nantucket-born Timothy G. Coffin, of New Bedford, bequeathed his comprehensive and valuable law library to the town of

Nantucket, with the proviso that the trustees of the Coffin School act as superintendents of the books. The will also stipulated that no one remove the books from the library, except judges in the Commonwealth and students of the Coffin School. The trustees authorized the town to locate the library in a room adjoining the selectmens' office, and appointed the librarians George Cobb, Esq., and, in 1874, Thaddeus G. Defriez.

After the school reopened in 1854, it averaged one hundred students between eight and twelve years old, per term, for several years. But by 1858, as the fortunes of the whale fishery declined, and as the island's public school system became more established, enrollment was down to an average of forty students per term. Elizabeth Crosby wrote to her sister in September 1858, "The tide of opinion now runs to the Public Schools and the Coffin School has few scholars."[5]

In 1862, as the island's economy languished in the shadow of the Civil War, the Coffin School trustees reduced the teachers' salaries, and in the same year the following short notice appeared in the paper to encourage parents to send their children to the school:

> Our patrons will see by the advertisement of the Coffin
> School that it commences a new quarter next week. This
> school offers many inducements for patronage. S.L. Meade
> the Principal, was for some years in one of the Public
> Schools, and a very successful teacher. For those who wish
> pupils prepared for the High School, this Institution offers
> great facilities. The number of pupils being less than that
> of the public schools, and the peculiar aptness of the
> principal and his thoroughness in teaching, and also his
> knowledge of the precise requirements of the committee for
> entrance into the High School, make the Coffin School an
> excellent one for the preparation above alluded to.[6]

In his memoir, Joseph Farnum recounted his days as a student at the school in the 1850s.[7] He was particularly fond of the Coffin School's principal, Alfred Macy, whom Farnum describes as "a young man of fine presence, of immaculate dress, always a gentleman, a cultured scholar, an excellent instructor, ever fair with his students, and he was beloved by all."[8] However, Farnum added, "A number of the boys in school sorely tried his patience and his temper."[9]

Farnum also recalled how, occasionally, during recess, students were given the unique privilege of looking through William Mitchell's telescope in his observatory, which stood in an open lot beyond the Coffin School yard. This appears to have been the same observatory that the Coffin School trustees had invited Maria Mitchell to build in 1859, on land west of the schoolhouse.[10]

The young Farnum paid for his tuition by working for David Folger, a dairy farmer on Gardner Street. He received fifty cents a week for driving Folger's cows home from a pasture beyond the Friends graveyard. Farnum remembered that one of Folger's daughters, Lydia, also studied at the Coffin School and later became a teacher there. "I can see her now, mentally, as she came forward to recite, and took a seat alone on the settee, she being the only student then in the 'classics.' "[11]

Tradition tells us that there was a spirit of rivalry between boys at the Coffin School and boys who attended the high school. There were apparently numerous incidences of fights between the "Coffin School proudies and the High School rowdies," as the two factions were called.[12] The Coffin School was often referred to as the school the island's "royal blue bloods" attended. For instance, a 1901 guidebook to the island, says the island's "Academy,–'the Coffin School'– incorporated eighty years ago, answers the question every intelligent visitor asks himself, 'Where do these insular people get such culture as they exhibit in wise speech and in refined, high bred manners?' "[13]

In the late 1860s, enrollment numbers improved at the school, approaching one hundred by 1870.[14] In the autumn of 1872, the school had reached capacity, and when Ellen B. Dunham, a Tuckernuck resident who boarded in town to attend school, applied for entrance, she was denied. She wrote to her family in January 1872: "I could not get into the Coffin School until the commencement of this term. The school was full, not one vacant seat, but this term he [E. B. Fox] said I could come in."[15] To accommodate the growth, the trustees employed additional teachers and erected a two-story addition to the rear of the original brick schoolhouse for the library and physical-science equipment. One thousand dollars was budgeted for the project, supervised by trustees Alfred Macy, Joseph Mitchell, and Charles G. Coffin.

The growth in enrollment may have been partly due to Edmund B. Fox, who became principal of the Coffin School in April 1869. When he was hired, a notice was placed in the *Inquirer and Mirror* stating that "Mr. Fox is a very superior teacher, and has a very high reputation where he has taught."[16] Under his tutelage, and that of his assistant Kate Macy, the school gained a reputation for fine scholarship. An advertisement in the 20 August 1892 issue of the *Inquirer and Mirror* boasted that graduates of the Coffin School had been "admitted to Cornell University, Brown University, Vassar College or Wellesley College on certificate."

Fox was considered a strict disciplinarian. As one trustee later noted, "His pupils early learned that his word was law, a law which must be obeyed."[17] His strictness may have gotten him in trouble with some of the students' parents. In the spring of 1881, a committee of trustees met on the subject of corporal punishment and wrote a letter to Fox informing him of their decision:

> That while it is the opinion of the committee that corporal punishment as a reformatory agent is a relic of past civilization, and not necessary for the government of a school, especially a private one, yet, taking into

consideration all the circumstances of the government of the Coffin School by the present principal; your committee would not recommend the abolishment of corporal punishment at this time, but would earnestly request the principal to reduce the number to the fewest possible.[18]

One of Fox's pupils, John Barreau, later recalled what it was like to be a student under Fox, whom he described as a "short somewhat stocky man" who was able to quash a revolt by the "big boys." He said the day began with all the students in the main room, the girls on one side and the boys on the other, and Principal Fox, with his three female assistant teachers, seated on the platform. After devotional exercises, the girls and their teachers would walk down the center aisle to classrooms in the rear. In addition, he remembered that "it was quite an event to be the boy whom Mr. Fox called in from play to ring the school bell which hung in a small cupola on the roof of the building. The bell rope was at the foot of the stairs leading to the attic at the top of which always stood a grinning skeleton used in the classes in physiology."[19]

Despite his severity, Fox was a devoted teacher and a friend to many of his students. At the end of each school year, he organized a school outing—called a levee—that consisted of a dance and refreshments. Barreau wrote that "One of the great events of school life was the annual school outing given by Mr. Fox. One year I particularly remember it was a trip to Wauwinet on the *Lillian* and another large cat-boat."[20] It was a memorable trip because on the voyage back to town it was discovered that two girls had been mistakenly left behind. After they were retrieved, one of the yachts ran aground. The evening, however, ended happily.

In July 1882, a guest who attended the Coffin School levee that year wrote a letter to the editor of the *Inquirer and Mirror*. He described the trip to Wauwinet House for an old-fashioned fish dinner, with the "joyful, healthy, fun-loving children huddled together in a boat." He recalled that the tables were elegantly set with "the whitest of cloths" and "a neatly printed bill of fare." After the dinner, he said, Benjamin B. Tobey got out his violin and Mrs. Frank B. Smith did the "calling."[21]

An indication of how much Edward Fox was admired by his students can be found in a notice in the *Inquirer and Mirror*, in 1872, in which it was reported that fifty of Fox's students braved a winter storm to surprise him on his thirtieth birthday: "Refreshments in profusion were contributed, and a general good time was enjoyed, in spite of the weather, which was a howling, smothering snow-storm, and so cold that *ice cream wouldn't freeze*."[22]

Among the assistants who served under Fox were Susan Coleman, Catherine Macy, Lydia M. Folger, Louise S. Baker, Elizabeth "Lizzie" S. Riddell, Eliza S. Paddack, Helen Marshall, Mary A. Greene, Gertrude M. King, Alice Coggeshall, Edith Cartwright, Libbie Marchant, Carrie Long, and Elma Folger.[23] When Louise S. Baker served as first assistant in the winter/spring term of 1871, one of her pupils described her as "splendid" and "such a reader, why when she is reading it sounds like a declamation."[24]

One of Fox's assistants who served the longest was Gertrude King, who taught at the Coffin School in the 1880s and 1890s. Born a Quaker on Nantucket, she studied at the normal school in Worcester, and taught in Greenfield before returning to Nantucket. In 1898 King had the distinction of being the Coffin School's only female principal, although her tenure lasted only for the final two terms that the school was open. Elma Folger was her assistant.

During this period, the school was supported partly by the income from its endowment and partly by tuition fees, which ranged between one and two dollars per term. For some families the cost was prohibitive. In a letter dated 15 July 1873, Captain Charles E. Allen, aboard the bark *Sea Ranger*, wrote to his daughter Lillian: "Father and Mother are willing you should go to the Coffin School and I hope we shall get an Extra Whale to pay for it."[25]

Graduations at the Coffin School were elaborate affairs, including scripture reading, songs, recitations of original declamations or essays, and musical solos on the violin or other instruments. The titles of some of the original declamations reflected the topics of the day. In July of 1884, Walter Coggeshall recited a piece he called "Shall Women Vote? No!!" and Ida S. Russell responded with a piece called "Shall Women Vote? Yes!!" A tradition had developed of displaying a class motto on the wall of the main room for the graduation ceremony.

Sir William Beechey's portrait of Admiral Coffin, which was purchased for the school in 1847, played a central role in graduations, when it was draped with an American flag. Even when graduations were held at the Atheneum, where there was more room, the portrait was moved there and festooned with the flag.

Examination days at the Coffin School were also important occasions for students, who were expected to wear their best attire. In December 1870, Ellen B. Dunham wrote "…mother it is pretty near examination day, at my school, and I have been thinking about it and it would seem queer for me to wear either of these dresses that the scholars have seen, every one has a new dress on that day, and it would seem queer for me not to."[26]

The teachers' record books dating to the mid- and late-nineteenth century include interesting notations regarding the classes and conduct of the students. Beginning in 1881, the ledgers recorded the "colored" scholars who enrolled in classes.[27] In the fall term of 1884, we find that George Lewis, aged fifteen, was discharged for truancy. During the winter term of 1885–86, Jessie Palmer, aged seventeen, the daughter of Virginia Quigley, was expelled because she was "vicious in conduct and a liar."[28]

Occasionally, the trustees of the Coffin School recorded the misconduct of students in the minutes of their meetings. At the 3 May 1877 meeting it was noted that "one of the scholars, Chas. F. Hammond, has been in the practice of using intoxicating liquor and thereby producing a bad influence upon other scholars."[29] The trustees voted to warn the student that the practice must discontinue or he would be expelled.

As early as 1855, the Coffin School trustees discussed establishing a music department, but it was not until the early 1870s that the study of music and singing was formally added to the curriculum. The school purchased a piano, and various instructors taught music over the years, including Martha Coleman, Isabelle Kingsbury, John Collins, and L.H. Johnson. In 1870 a telescope was purchased for the school; in the 1880s, astronomy and drawing classes were added to the curriculum, and in 1892–93 botany was offered.

In the early 1880s, the school seems to have experienced a kind of renaissance. On 24 July 1880, the *Inquirer and Mirror* noted that under Fox's care as principal, "seconded by an able corps of assistants [the Coffin School] has become a popular seminary of learning, and is in every respect an ornament to the town." In 1881, George H. Folger (who had attended the school in 1828–29) commented: "While disasters and misfortunes without number have fallen thick and heavy upon the old town, while her children have been driven to the ends of the earth to earn a livelihood, while her wharves have fallen in decay, the grass grown in her streets, and the sound of labor become low or ceased altogether, yet this grand old institution, founded in love and good will, standing almost alone, has flourished and grown strong amid a general wreck."[30]

In 1884 the students started up a paper, the *Coffin School Record,* which featured essays, poems, notes on alumni, and editorial comments and anecdotes. In the June issue of that year the students wrote, "We shall endeavor to so blend Religious, instructive, laughable and local matter, as to make our paper so interesting that it will be indispensable to both the old and young in every house-hold." Story topics ranged from the sad death of two classmates, who drowned off Coatue, to the train conductor who was fired after he left a load of passengers waiting impatiently in town as he enjoyed his clam dinner in Surfside. In the column "Odds and Ends" in the same issue we find comments like "The rotating swing in our yard is a never failing source of amusement to the boys" and "The pupils have named the street on which the school house stands Crescent Avenue, but we think Crescent River would be more appropriate in wet weather."

In the December issue we learn that "The political complexion of this school is decidedly of one hue, there being but one Democrat among our number." The alumni notes indicate that a large number of Coffin School graduates went on to further study or teaching positions.

Despite the Coffin School's active programs, enrollment continued to decline as Nantucket's year-round population dwindled to three thousand residents. In the 1897–98 academic year, only thirty pupils were enrolled, and the school's income had decreased dramatically. With Nantucket's still-fledgling tourist economy unable to fill the void left by the demise of the whale fishery, fewer and fewer families were able to afford the costs of tuition and books. In January 1898 the illness and resignation of Edward B. Fox, who had guided the school as teacher and principal for twenty-nine years, brought the situation to a crisis. Gertrude King stepped in for the remaining two terms of the school year, but by the summer the trustees had closed the doors on the Greek Revival building.

Fig. 17 Josiah Freeman, *The Coffin School*, ca. 1870. This rare early image of Coffin School students in front of the newly built schoolhouse on Winter Street was taken by Josiah Freeman. A native of New Bedford, Freeman spent much of his life in Nantucket, where he established a photography studio on Main Street. *Courtesy of the Nantucket Historical Association.*

Fig. 18 *Alfred and Anne Mitchell Macy*, ca. 1850s. When the Coffin School's new Greek Revival brick building opened in 1854 on Winter Street, Alfred Macy served as the first principal. A former student of his, Joseph Farnum, recalled that Mr. Macy was a "a young man of fine presence, of immaculate dress, always a gentleman, a cultured scholar, an excellent instructor, ever fair with his students, and he was beloved by all." In 1857 he married Anne Mitchell (see inset), sister of famed astronomer Maria Mitchell. Anne taught languages at the Coffin School from 1854–57. Macy resigned his position in the spring of 1861 to practice law, and he became a Coffin School trustee in the fall of that same year. *Photographs courtesy of the Nantucket Historical Association.*

Fig. 19 *Coffin School Bell*, ca. 1854, bronze and wood. The bell was produced at the brass foundry on South Beach Street, established in 1821 by Benjamin Field and Peleg Macy. Decorated with swags, stars, and hearts, the bell was made for the Greek Revival Coffin School on Winter Street. It was considered a great privilege for a child to be chosen by the principal to ring the bell, which hung in the small cupola on the roof of the building. *Courtesy of the Nantucket Historical Association.*

Fig. 20 *Coffin School Students,* 1884. Sometime in the late nineteenth century it became a tradition to display class mottoes on the schoolroom wall. For the class of 1884 it was "*Chacun est artisan de sa fortune,*" which means "Everyone is the maker of his or her own fortune." *Courtesy of the Nantucket Historical Association.*

Fig. 21 *Edmund B. Fox,* ca. 1870. He served as principal of the Coffin School from 1869 until the school's closing in 1898. Although considered a strict disciplinarian, he was much admired by his students. The school flourished under his direction and gained a reputation for fine scholarship. *Courtesy of the Nantucket Historical Association.*

Fig. 22 *The Coffin School with Students*, ca. 1880. The Coffin School went through a kind of renaissance in the early 1880s, with students involved in various new activities including a military company with drills led by Major Albert B. Holmes, a chorus that sang gospel songs and glees for a Temperance Society benefit, and a student newspaper called the *Coffin School Record. Courtesy of the Nantucket Historical Association.*

Fig. 23 *Gertrude King*, ca. 1885. One of Edward B. Fox's assistants, Gertrude King taught at the Coffin School in the 1880s and 1890s. Born a Quaker on Nantucket, she studied at the normal school in Worcester and taught in Greenfield before returning to the island. She has the distinction of being the Coffin School's only woman principal, a position she held in the last two terms before the school closed in 1898. Like Elizabeth R. Coffin, she was a strong advocate for reopening the school as an industrial-arts school. *Courtesy of the Nantucket Historical Association.*

4

Manual Training & Home Economics: 1903–1930s

Following the closing of the school in 1898, there was much speculation as to its fate. The summer after the closing, Elizabeth Rebecca Coffin, an accomplished artist, part-time island resident, and granddaughter of Gorham Coffin–one of the school's first trustees– wrote to the Coffin School trustees. She recommended that the school be reopened to offer manual-training courses in conjunction with the public school system. Coffin's ideas reflected those of the then-burgeoning Arts and Crafts movement in America, which advocated a revival of handcrafted furniture and objects and the building up of village industries.

In 1902, Coffin fully outlined her vision for the school:

> I find that in all educational centres there has been a remarkable growth in appreciation of the importance of

manual training. It has been made part of the system of
education in all our large cities and skilled educators lay the
greatest stress on the value of the training of mind and
hand and eye by actual mechanical work.... There have
been a number of successful experiments in small towns by
which the introduction of handicrafts has provided
wholesome occupation for the inhabitants and has become
a source of revenue to them, work done during the winter
months finding a ready market with summer visitors and in
the world at large. ...Manual training leading to such
handicrafts would be particularly useful in Nantucket and
would be of practical value to young people....[1]

Coffin firmly believed the course of action she recommended would
have met with Admiral Sir Isaac Coffin's approval, as he once expressed
the wish that the school should give a "practical" education.[2]

By September, Elizabeth Coffin had taken a step toward the
realization of her goal for the school. Along with Coffin School alumni
and Coffin family members, she founded the Coffin School Association
to maintain a spirit of fellowship among those who had studied at the
school, to promote the interests of the Coffin School, and to help
increase its endowment fund. In 1909 the association was incorporated.[3]

The trustees eventually followed Elizabeth Coffin's advice. With the
assistance of the Coffin School Association, combined with the income
from the school's endowment, the trustees reopened the school on 5
October 1903 as a manual-training department for the public schools.
By that date, manual training as part of public education had spread to
most cities in the state.[4] To allow for the changes, the Massachusetts
legislature passed an amendment to the Coffin School's charter. For the
first time in its history, the school did not charge tuition fees; all
expenses were paid for by the endowment fund. With great pride, the
local paper reported that "After a silence of about five years, the Coffin
School bell sounded natural, as it pealed forth a welcome to pupils,

Monday morning. Long live the Coffin School and its bell!"[5]

In the summer months preceding the opening date, the main room was renovated with a new hard-pine floor, fresh paint on the walls, and twenty maple woodworking benches equipped with joiners tools. The *Inquirer and Mirror* reported that the remodeled assembly room "With its fine proportions and harmonious colors it is one of the most beautiful rooms devoted to its purpose in the country."[6]

The manual-training equipment was donated by Elizabeth Coffin in memory of her father, Andrew G. Coffin, who had been born on Nantucket. She gave the equipment with the stipulation that she could put up a tablet honoring her father, and that the courses be offered to both boys and girls. She modeled the tablet herself and had it cast in bronze.

George M. Morris of Dorchester, Massachusetts, was hired as the first manual-training teacher.[7] Students (boys and girls) in grades nine through twelve spent one full session a week learning woodworking and mechanical drawing. Morris's instruction followed the Swedish *Sloyd* system of hand training, "which trains in concentration of mind and accuracy of thought and execution by awakening interest in an object of practical use rather than by giving abstract exercises."[8]

In January 1904, the building was wired for electric lights–also paid for by Elizabeth Coffin–allowing the school to offer special evening classes. Attended by young men and boys, the evening classes eventually included instruction in mechanical drawing, joinery, cabinet work, and wood-turning. Students learned the principles of craftsmanship and to make furniture and other useful objects, mostly in the Arts and Crafts style. The ultimate goal of the advanced classes was to assist men and boys on the island to become carpenters and cabinetmakers.

In addition to woodworking, industrial basketry classes were offered for girls and boys several afternoons and in the evenings.[9] Taught by Julia Farrington, the course was open to the public and cost fifty cents plus materials. An article in the *Inquirer and Mirror* of 17 September 1904 explained: "The courses in basketry…are offered in hope that they may be the beginning of a small household industry for some Nantucketers who have leisure hours through the winter. There is constant inquiry on the part of summer visitors for articles of island manufacture…. Miss Farrington has worked out a course in woven basketry which…should enable her pupils to meet this demand…. The course in sewed basketry for advanced pupils should enable them to produce baskets which rank as works of art."

In a promotional leaflet given out by the Coffin School Association in 1906, president Fred Fuller reported that "a village industry" was developing out of the industrial basketry classes initiated in 1904. He claimed that "Out of some 200 baskets made during the first school year, all but four were sold during the summer of 1905, with considerable profit to those who made them. The Coffin School has begun a work of inestimable value to Nantucket, and its new departure has called forth tokens of approval from many sources."

During the first years after the school reopened, articles in the local paper stated that the Coffin School was a great asset to the community. The reporters boasted that not only did the students become skillful workers at home, they were also able to enter technical schools off-island. George H. Martin, secretary of the State Board of Education, spoke on the value of handwork at the Coffin School Association's annual meeting in August 1905 and stated that "the Coffin School is doing as important a work as it ever did in the days of the island's prosperity." [10]

However, comments by Fred V. Fuller, president of the Coffin School Association, indicate that not everyone approved of the school's new mission. In an address to the association on 27 August 1909, Fuller paid tribute to George Morris, who was leaving his post as principal, and said: "Whatever results those who follow him may achieve, we shall always remember that he had to blaze the way, overcome distrust and inertia, and win through his work those who dubbed the project 'a whittling school' at the very start." [11]

Over the years, as new equipment was purchased or given to the school, the scope of the manual-training classes expanded. In 1905, William Watson, who had attended the Coffin School as a child, gave the school four wood-turning lathes with tools. In 1907 and 1908, additional tools enabled the school to teach metalwork in copper, brass, tin, and steel, plus patternmaking, forging, and moulding. With these additions, "The facilities of the school now compare well with those of technical schools elsewhere," said George Morris in his 1908 report to the town.[12] In 1911, a gas engine and a table saw were installed, and by 1921, blueprint reading was offered. As Elizabeth Rebecca Coffin told the Coffin School Association in August 1910, expansion of the courses offered was needed because "this school can give the fundamental training which fits a boy quickly to acquire any trade."[13]

Beginning in February 1905, again due to the influence of Elizabeth Coffin, the Coffin School trustees began offering instruction in sewing once a week to girls in grades eight through twelve. The classes were held in the library on the second floor, which had been renovated for this use with funds provided by Maria Tallant Owen, in memory of her grandfather William Coffin, first president of the board of trustees (a tablet with a commemorative inscription still hangs in the room). An elaborate bookcase was constructed on one side of the room, a memorial for the library donated by Frances Mitchell Macy, daughter of Alfred and Anne Mitchell Macy, both former teachers in the Coffin School.[14] For the sewing classes, cane chairs and specially made seven-foot-long oak tables with inlaid yardsticks were purchased from a firm in Boston, and can still be seen in the Coffin School today.

Nantucket native Charlotte Miller Coffin, wife of Charles Henry Coffin, was hired as the sewing teacher, a position she held until 1913.[15] She initiated a graded system of sewing, which she had previously introduced in the Somerville schools. Under her tutelage, the girls, varying in number from ten to twenty-four students, were furnished with blank books in which they wrote down sewing instructions and illustrated each lesson with a model. The models systematically taught the different stitches, including darning, patching, etc. In her report to the school committee in 1905, Charlotte Coffin wrote that the books show the "neatness and intelligence in needlework, training of the eye and hand, and an artistic sense." [16] Many of the notebooks survive today, having been handed down to family members or donated to public collections on the island. These charming schoolgirl books, with their neat handwriting and tiny examples of stitches, were much cherished items. Harriet Barnard (Barrett) Fleming, in her *Reminiscences, 1903–1909*, wrote, "On Friday afternoon we went to the Coffin School…. May I boast to say, that I made the best darning…in the class." [17]

The models were followed by practical work in making articles of clothing, varying in degree of difficulty depending on the age of the student. Among the articles made: plain and fancy aprons, short skirts, white skirts with flounces, kimonos, infants dresses, and shirtwaists–hand-embroidered, tucked, and trimmed. In 1907 a Singer sewing machine was purchased, and that same year a class in applied design, taught with the assistance of May Congdon, was added to the girls courses.

In June of 1905, the school began the tradition of holding a public exhibition day when examples of student work were put on display. A portion of the day was devoted to watching the boys and girls working at their benches. In later years, the *Inquirer and Mirror* published lengthy lists of the items on view. For instance, in 1914, the objects displayed included bookends, "Morris" chairs, tables, record cabinets, umbrella stands, footstools, folding screens, trays, and cedar chests. For sewing, the items displayed included aprons, corset covers, pillow slips, dresses, skirts, embroidered night robes, blouses, and doll outfits. Often the exhibit was open throughout the summer and, according to the local press, attracted considerable attention. Much of the work shown, especially the basketry, was offered for sale, and duplicates of furniture made by the boys could be ordered.

It was also in 1905, through donations by Mrs. Mildram, Mrs. William F. Macy, and Charles C. Barrett, that a fine collection of plaster casts was purchased for the school. Elizabeth Coffin went to the P. P. Capproni & Brother showroom in Boston to make the selections. She chose casts that were "reproductions of celebrated works of sculpture and were selected with care to illustrate as wide a range as possible of the world's history and art."[18] Three of the casts are still on display in the main hall today: two portions of the frieze from the Parthenon and a large Assyrian panel representing a king hunting lions.[19] As the local paper suggested, the donors of the casts hoped they would be of "inestimable value in cultivating the taste of our young people."[20]

In July of 1914 the Coffin School Association established another annual tradition that became a community event: Garden Day. The events were generally organized by Elizabeth Coffin, who sometimes on her own veranda at her home on Lily Street offered tea or a talk on art, as part of the festivities. Begun as a fund-raiser, the first Garden Days consisted of tours of gardens, the sale of flowers, and the serving of tea. Eventually, the event became a full-fledged community fair, offering games, art exhibitions, pony cart rides, singing, dramatic readings, an auction, music, baked goods, and more. Among the notable special events were performances by the Sea Cliff Inn Orchestra in the early 1920s and a marionette show performed by Tony Sarg in 1937. In 1923, the local paper noted the popularity of the Garden Day, claiming that it was an "event in which the whole Island (resident and visitor) joins to show its interest in and loyalty to this fundamental project for the good of the whole community."[21]

With funds raised by the Coffin School Association, and additional generous bequests and gifts, in 1918 an addition was built at the rear of the main schoolhouse in order to provide instruction in home economics for girls.[22] On 22 August 1918, the opening of the new addition was celebrated with singing by the high school chorus in the Methodist Church, followed by a procession up Liberty Street, which had been decorated with Chinese lanterns for the occasion. According to one report, "The new room designed for the teaching of Home Economics is most admirably suited to the purpose. Careful attention has been given to all the details, and the result is a room well lighted, heated, ventilated, and sanitary in every particular. The equipment is of the most modern type, and has been installed with the object of giving the very best of everything to the teachers and scholars."[23]

The first head instructor of the home economics program was Mrs. Earle H. Meyer, a graduate of Stout Institute in Menominee, Wisconsin. She was followed in succession by Lelia Coffin Williams, Ethel Weeks, Ida Harper, Sarah Packard, again Lelia Williams—now Mrs. Earl S. Ray, and Grace Helfer Holdgate.[24] In the late 1930s, the school began the tradition of annual fashion shows in June to exhibit the girls' sewing work.

The home economics courses followed the trend in high schools at that time to teach girls "the essential facts on which the health and well-being of the family depend."[25] A science that had developed in the early years of the twentieth century, home economics included courses in child care, cooking, sewing, nutrition, and etiquette.

Also in 1918, Alvin E. Paddock, an island carpenter who had renovated the floors of the school before it reopened in 1903, was hired as principal and manual training teacher, positions he held until September 1941.[26] Beginning in 1913, he also served as one of the Coffin School trustees. In 1954, the room he used at the school was renovated and officially named the Paddock Room.

In 1924, the students' work at the Coffin School became an integral part of the public school system, counting toward a diploma. Students were given one point of credit toward graduation for each year's work at the Coffin School. In October of that year, the Coffin School Association handed over to the trustees $45,000 toward an endowment to ensure the home economics classes would continue.

Fig. 24 *Elizabeth Rebecca Coffin*, ca. 1910. Born in Brooklyn, New York, Elizabeth R. Coffin (1851–1930) was the daughter of Elizabeth Sherwood of New York and Andrew G. Coffin of Nantucket. After becoming an accomplished artist, she eventually moved to Nantucket, where she lived at 23 Lily Street. After the Coffin School closed its doors in 1898, Elizabeth persuaded the trustees to reopen the school as a manual-training and home economics center for the public school system. For close to thirty years she devoted much of her time to raising funds for the school. When she died on Nantucket in 1930, the Coffin School Association established a memorial to her in the form of a scholarship, and a bronze plaque in her honor was placed in the main room in 1931. *Courtesy of the Nantucket Historical Association.*

Fig. 25 Elizabeth Rebecca Coffin, *Self-Portrait*, ca. 1890, oil on canvas. Elizabeth Coffin studied painting and drawing at The Hague Academy of Fine Arts in the Netherlands, and later at the Brooklyn Art Guild and the Pennsylvania Academy of Fine Arts with renowned artist Thomas Eakins. She exhibited her paintings, many of them Nantucket subjects, at the National Academy of Design and Brooklyn Art Association. The Coffin School Trustees own many fine examples of her work. *Collection of the Coffin School Trustees.*

Fig. 26 Thomas Eakins, *Portrait of Elizabeth Rebecca Coffin*, ca. 1900, oil on canvas. Elizabeth Coffin remained a friend and colleague of Thomas Eakins for many years. This striking, intimate portrait of her is a testament to that close friendship. *Collection of the Coffin School Trustees.*

Fig. 27 *Coffin School Interior*, ca. 1905. Twenty maple woodworking benches and joiners tools for the manual-training classes were donated by Elizabeth Rebecca Coffin in memory of her father, Andrew G. Coffin. Visible on the rear wall are the portraits of William Coffin, Admiral Sir Isaac Coffin, and Lieut. Alexander Pinkham. The former two still hang in the main hall today. *Courtesy of the Nantucket Historical Association.*

Fig. 28 *Coffin School Interior*, ca. 1905. Visible in this photograph are some of the pieces of furniture made in the manual-training class in the then-popular Arts and Crafts style. The plaster casts of classical reliefs on the back wall were given to the school in 1905 as teaching tools for art and history and to cultivate the taste of the young students. *Courtesy of the Nantucket Historical Association.*

Fig. 29 *Coffin School Cooking Class*, 1924. When this photograph was taken, Ethel Weeks was the home economics instructor. Cooking classes at that time included learning to prepare food for home and school, and menus and table service. The girls are, left to right: Margaret Dunham, Alice Duce, Harriet Chadwick, Priscilla Coleman, Lillian Burchell, Laura Foster, Catherine Ray, Grace Holden, Catherine Sylvia, Dorothy Gardner, Frances Terry, Elizabeth Norcross, Florence Barrett, Frances Sylvia, Magdeline Sousa, and Madeline Voorneveld. *Collection of the Coffin School Trustees.*

Fig. 30 *Sewing Class Display*, ca. 1925. Beginning in June 1904, the Coffin School held public exhibitions every summer to display and sell examples from the manual-training and home economics classes. The exhibits were well attended by the community. *Collection of the Coffin School Trustees.*

Fig. 31 Jessie Tarbox Beals, *Garden Day: Donkey Rides*, 1916. During a short visit to Nantucket, Jessie Tarbox Beals, America's first woman photojournalist, took a series of photographs of the Coffin School's Garden Day festivities on August 4, 1916. Originally begun as a fund-raiser, the event eventually became a full-fledged community fair with pony-cart rides, art exhibitions, games, musical performances, and more. *Collection of the Coffin School Trustees.*

Fig. 32 Jessie Tarbox Beals, *Garden Day: Races*, 1916. The three-legged race was one of the festivities offered for children at the 1916 Garden Day. Note the line of pony carts along Winter Street, waiting to head off for a tour of the island. *Collection of the Coffin School Trustees.*

Fig. 33 Jessie Tarbox Beals, *Garden Day: Story-time*, 1916. One of the favorite features of the Garden Day fairs was storytelling. In this photograph, Henry Harmon Chamberlin reads stories to children on the lawn of the Swift home, next door to the Coffin School. *Collection of the Coffin School Trustees.*

Fig. 34 *Alvin E. Paddock*, ca. 1940. In 1918, Alvin Paddock, an island carpenter, was hired as principal and manual-training teacher at the Coffin School, positions he held until 1941. In 1954, a room he used at the rear of the school was remodeled and named the Paddock Room in his honor. *Collection of the Coffin School Trustees.*

Fig. 35 *Lelia Coffin Williams Ray,* ca. 1925. After attending Nantucket High School, including sewing and manual-training classes at the Coffin School, Lelia studied at Framingham Normal School. For several years before her marriage in 1924, she taught household arts at the Coffin School. She returned in 1943 as teacher of the food courses and in 1945 became director of the home economics department. Later she also taught sewing. *Courtesy of the Nantucket Historical Association.*

5

Serving the Community: 1940s–Present

In 1940, the Coffin School trustees found that they were once again facing financial difficulties. For numerous decades they had provided Nantucket children with free instruction in manual training and domestic science. Despite generous contributions from the Coffin School Association, effects of the Depression had been such that the school was operating at a deficit in the mid to late 1930s. The type of instruction being offered by the school was now required by the Commonwealth of Massachusetts. To reduce the economic drain on the endowment, in the spring of 1941 the Coffin School's courses became more fully integrated into the public high school curriculum. The Nantucket School Committee arranged to rent Coffin School facilities for a state-aided, vocational school for the boys.[1] The committee also paid for the teachers and materials.

Under the auspices of the high school, Thomas McAuley taught the metalwork classes, and Leroy True taught woodworking. The new plan required the boys to spend more hours in the shop (twenty-one hours a week, rather than eight), and, instead of only making objects to take home with them, they were given projects to undertake for the public schools' properties and programs. Among the objects they made in the 1940s were a bicycle rack, shelves, a fence, oak tables, lawn chairs, book cabinets, bulletin boards, music stands, and scenery for the school plays.

The domestic science classes continued to be offered by the Coffin School Trustees and were taught by Grace Helfer Holdgate (hand and machine sewing), and Lelia Coffin Williams Ray (nutrition and cooking). The girls contributed items to the town; during wartime they aided the Red Cross in making children's garments and learned to economize in cooking because of rationing. Under the new system, the Coffin School continued to present student exhibitions, including fashion shows for the sewing classes, and the Coffin School Association continued to sponsor fund-raising events.

Many of the handcrafted objects made at the Coffin School have been handed down in families on the island as treasured items. David D. Worth, class of 1946 and formerly manager of the Wannacomet Water Company, still has the small wooden stool he made, and he recalls with pride a wine goblet with a delicate stem that he constructed of mahogany. Jane Richmond, class of 1947, has the chip-carved desk set (ink stand and pen tray) made in 1914 by her mother–the multitalented Lelia Coffin Williams Ray–as well as samples of her own sewing done at the school in the 1940s.

In 1968, an addition to the high school resulted in the complete relocation of the vocational and home economics programs from the Coffin School to Nantucket High School. Grace Helfer (formerly Grace Holdgate), home economics teacher, and Patrick Paradis and Thomas McAuley, both shop teachers, carried on the courses formerly offered at the Coffin School. The Coffin School's role in educating several generations of skilled island tradespeople–including carpenters, cabinetmakers, painters, electricians, builders, contractors, mechanics, dressmakers, basket weavers, and caterers–had ended.

After serving the needs of the island community as an educational institution for more than a century, a new era began for the Coffin School. Beginning in the late 1960s, seminars, courses, lectures, demonstrations, musical events, and other programs were presented at the school under the auspices of different island and off-island nonprofit organizations, including the University of Massachusetts, Cape Cod Community College, the Maria Mitchell Association, the Artists' Association of Nantucket, the Nantucket Chamber Music Center, Preservation Institute: Nantucket, and the Nantucket Learning and Resource Center.

From 1969 until 1978, the Nantucket public school's kindergarten, under the direction of Jane Lamb, occupied the rear rooms on the first floor and the library on the second floor, and renovations to the building were made to accommodate the children.

In 1970, the Massachusetts legislature passed an act to change the Coffin School's charter to read that the Admiral Sir Isaac Coffin's Lancasterian School may "advance, promote, aid, give or furnish education of any kind deemed desirable by the Trustees, for any or all seasons of the year."[2] This enabled the school to offer classes at any level. For instance, in the summer of 1970, the University of Massachusetts-Boston presented the Nantucket Summer Institute, a four-credit course.

Although dusty chalkboards no longer grace its walls, and oak desks or woodworking benches no longer crowd the main room, the Coffin School continues to offer the Nantucket community enriching and diverse educational programs. Today the building is home to the Egan Institute of Maritime Studies, which was founded in 1996 to advance the scholarly study and appreciation of the history, literature, art, and maritime traditions of Nantucket Island. In addition to sponsoring research, educational programs, exhibitions, and publications, the Egan Institute seeks to perpetuate the legacy of the school's founder, Admiral Sir Isaac Coffin, through its support of nautical training for the youth of Nantucket.

Today, Nantucket Island Community Sailing (NICS), with offices in the lower level of the school, offers sailing instruction for children and adults at a reasonable cost. Together, the Egan Institute and NICS sponsor the Admiral's Cup, an annual dinghy race.

The Coffin School continues to serve the educational and cultural needs of the island by offering use of its exquisitely restored main hall to various island organizations for concerts, seminars, lectures, and other programs. The school's trustees annually award scholarships to graduating high school seniors for further study.

Although it has undergone many changes over the last one hundred and seventy one years, the Coffin School remains a fitting memorial to the beneficence of its founder, Admiral Sir Isaac Coffin.

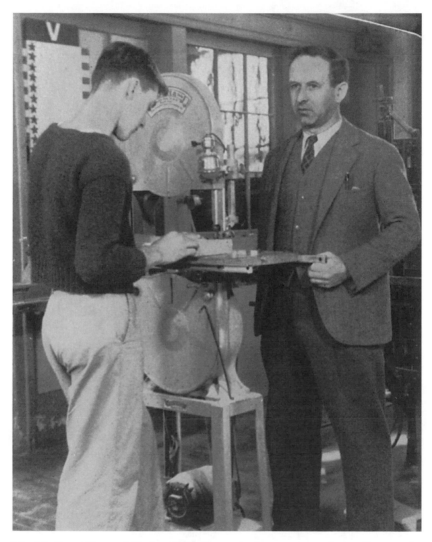

Fig. 36 *Leroy True and Student,* 1945. For more than ten years, Leroy True taught woodworking classes and was principal of Nantucket High School's industrial-arts program at the Coffin School. From 1974–83, he served as president of the Nantucket Historical Association. *Reproduced from the Nantucket High School yearbook, 1945.*

Figs. 37 *Metalwork Class,* 1944. The metalwork classes of the high school's industrial-arts program were taught in the basement of the Coffin School. The table on which the students are working eventually was used in the Nantucket Atheneum as the periodical table. Today it is once again found in the basement of the Coffin School. *Reproduced from the Nantucket High School Yearbook, 1944.*

Fig. 38 *Sarah Alice Packard and Students*, 1945. Educated at Bridgewater Normal School and Simmons College, Sarah Packard served as head of the home economics department at the Coffin School from 1931 to 1945. In 1932, she initiated an annual fashion show at which her girls modeled dresses they had made in her classes. Her students also presented an annual tea or banquet to which guests from the community were invited. *Reproduced from the Nantucket High School yearbook, 1945.*

Fig. 39 *Coffin School Boys*, 1944. The vocational arts boys carry on the tradition of posing on the steps of the Coffin School. By this date, the program was fully integrated with the public school system. *Reproduced from the Nantucket High School yearbook, 1944.*

NOTES

Chapter 1

ADMIRAL SIR ISAAC COFFIN

1 Nathaniel Philbrick, *Admiral Sir Isaac Coffin, Baronet: The Vicarious Nantucketer*, 1992, video typescript, p. 2.

2 Thomas Coffin Amory, *The Life of Admiral Sir Isaac Coffin, Baronet* (Boston: Cupples, Upham & Co., 1886), 33.

3 Joseph C. Hart, *Miriam Coffin or The Whale-Fishermen* (1834; Nantucket, MA: Mill Hill Press, 1995), 337. Hart dedicated this book to "his friend" the admiral.

4 Philbrick, p. 3.

5 *The Naval Chronicle* 12 (1804), 12.

6 Amory, p. 48.

7 A notice in the *Inquirer* of 16 September 1826 suggests this was his second trip to the island, the first having occurred twenty years previously.

8 Ibid.

9 Amory, p. 61. The admiral gave one medal to each of the trustees of the Coffin School in 1828; the one for the president was gilt. According to tradition, a young man stole the medal, believing it was solid gold. When he tried to melt it down he was disappointed to find that there was brass beneath. Allen Coffin wrote that when the admiral was a guest of Captain Alex Coffin at Hudson, New York, he had a bag of these medals that he left with the

captain. See Allen Coffin to Susan Starbuck, 8 March 1898, Nantucket Schools Collection, Nantucket Historical Association.

10 *Inquirer and Mirror,* 18 May 1872.

11 William Coffin to Sir Isaac Coffin, 1 November 1826, copy in *Records of Admiral Sir Isaac Coffin's Lancasterian School,* Collection of the Coffin School Trustees.

12 Admiral Coffin to William Coffin, 20 March 1827, Admiral Sir Isaac Coffin's Lancasterian School Papers, Nantucket Historical Association.

13 *Inquirer and Mirror,* 17 March 1917.

14 According to Nathaniel Philbrick.

15 George H. Folger to Charles G. Coffin, 30 June 1881, published in Amory, p. 110.

Chapter 2
THE EARLY YEARS: 1827–1846

1 Other principals of the school during the early years were J. H. Warland, William H. Wood, Augustus Morse, Hiram B. Dennis, Frederick Vinton, and William H. Hewes. Assistants over this period were Andrew M. Macy, Mary Folger, Lydia Fowler, Charlotte Clasby, Mary Clisby, Caroline Austin, Phebe Clisby, Nancy Luce, Avis Gardner, and Elizabeth Easton.

2 Obituary, *Nantucket Inquirer,* 2 May 1838. He served as preceptor through June 1834.

3 These plaster casts of the admiral were taken from a marble bust made by William Behnes in 1826 and given to the Boston Athenaeum by the admiral in 1827.

4 William Coffin to Admiral Coffin, 9 December 1827, Admiral Sir Isaac Coffin's Lancasterian School Papers, Nantucket Historical Association.

5 Admiral Coffin to William Coffin, 29 December 1827, Admiral Sir Isaac Coffin's Lancasterian School Papers, Nantucket Historical Association. Other tokens of merit awarded were watches for boys and rings for girls.

6 Coffin School Record Book 1834-1837, Nantucket Schools Collection, Nantucket Historical Association.

7 Coffin School Record Book 51, 1837-1839, Coffin School Papers, Nantucket Historical Association.

8 Samuel H. Jenks to W.R.E., 1859, printed in the *Inquirer and Mirror,* date unknown, Nantucket Historical Association (Blue Files).

9 *Nantucket Inquirer,* 11 September 1839.

10 Obed Macy Journal, July 1822–October 1827, Macy Family Papers, Nantucket Historical Association.

11 Admiral Coffin to William Coffin, 30 November 1828, Admiral Sir Isaac Coffin's Lancasterian School Papers, Nantucket Historical Association.

12 The admiral had originally planned to establish three nautical schools: one at Boston, one at Newburyport, and one at Nantucket. Only the Nantucket school materialized.

13 Will Gardner, *The Coffin Saga* (Cambridge, MA: The Riverside Press, 1949), 213–14.

14 Admiral Coffin to William Coffin, 16 September 1829, copy in *Records of Admiral Sir Isaac Coffin's Lancasterian School*, Collection of the Coffin School Trustees.

15 *Inquirer and Mirror*, 13 May 1893.

16 Captain Pinkham to William Coffin, 23 May 1830, typescript copy in Ships' Papers Collection, Nantucket Historical Association, original at William L. Clements Library, Ann Arbor, Michigan.

17 *Nantucket Inquirer*, 8 August 1829.

18 Ibid.

19 Ibid.

20 Ibid., 15 August 1829.

21 Admiral Coffin to "Gentlemen" (the trustees), 1 January 1832, Admiral Sir Isaac Coffin's Lancasterian School Papers, Nantucket Historical Association.

22 Admiral Coffin to trustees of the Coffin School, 24 June 1835, Admiral Sir Isaac Coffin's Lancasterian School Papers, Nantucket Historical Association.

23 *Nantucket Inquirer*, 12 March 1831.

24 Gorham Coffin to Admiral Coffin, 12 January 1836, Admiral Sir Isaac Coffin's Lancasterian School Papers, Nantucket Historical Association.

25 Masonic Fund Record Book, n.p., Collection of the Coffin School Trustees.

26 Masonic Fund Record Book, p. 13, Collection of the Coffin School Trustees.

27 A copy of the portrait by Stuart exists, but remains unlocated. It is not known if the copy was done by Stuart or another hand.

28 Godfrey, Edward K., *The Island of Nantucket, What It Was And What It Is* (Boston: Lee and Shepard, Publishers, 1882): 20–21.

Chapter 3
A NEW GREEK REVIVAL HOME: 1854–1898

1 On 25 March 1859 and 29 January 1862, the trustees put notices in the *Inquirer* offering a reward for information about "the person or persons who threw down and broke the iron gate in front of the Coffin School House."

2 Coffin School Account Book 1846–1873, Coffin School Papers, Nantucket

Historical Association. The book also includes the names of various workmen who constructed the building, including Noah Poole, a mason; Charles H. Robinson, a builder and marble artisan; Mitchell & Austin, tin and iron workers; Charles and Daniel Clark, masons; and Gustavus Gifford, a blacksmith. Suppliers are also listed, like Tufts & Boyden and B. & J. Folger–bricks; R. Hallet–stone; and A. H. Robinson–marble.

3 According to Helen Wright in *Sweeper in the Sky* (New York: The Macmillan Company, 1949), 56, Anne was known on the island as the "mistress of seven foreign tongues." Anne attended the Coffin School in the 1830s.

4 Alfred Macy to the Coffin School Trustees, 13 April 1861, copy in Coffin School Trustees Record Book, 1847–1884, Collection of the Coffin School Trustees.

5 Elizabeth (Pinkham) Crosby to Malvina Pinkham, 2 September 1858, Marshall, Pinkham Family Papers, Nantucket Historical Association.

6 *Nantucket Inquirer,* 22 January 1862.

7 Joseph Farnum, *Brief Historical Data and Memories of My Boyhood Days in Nantucket* (Providence, R.I.: Snow & Farnham Company, 1915), 45-48.

8 Ibid., p. 46.

9 Ibid.

10 Coffin School Trustees Meeting Minutes, 29 January 1859, Coffin School Trustees Record Book, 1847–1884, n.p., Collection of the Coffin School Trustees. The land to the west of the school was sold in 1866.

11 Farnum, p. 129.

12 *Inquirer and Mirror,* 28 July 1923.

13 A. Judd Northrup, 'S*conset Cottage Life: A Summer On Nantucket Island* (Syracuse, New York: C.W. Bardeen, Publisher, 1901), 89-90.

14 In 1874 the trustees decided to limit the enrollment to one hundred students per term.

15 Ellen B. Dunham to "The Folks at Home," 21 January 1872, Collection of William and Ruth Grieder, Nantucket.

16 *Inquirer and Mirror,* 6 January 1869.

17 Handwritten biography of Fox, Nantucket Historical Association (Blue Files).

18 Thaddeus Defriez and David Folger to Mr. E. B. Fox, 22 April 1881, Coffin School Papers, Nantucket Historical Association.

19 *Inquirer and Mirror,* 11 September 1943.

20 Ibid.

21 Ibid., 8 July 1882.

22 Ibid., 9 March 1872.

23 During most terms there were a first assistant, a second assistant, and a third assistant.

24 Ellen B. Dunham to Mrs. James Dunham, 9 March 1871, Collection of William and Ruth Grieder, Nantucket. Beginning in 1879, Louise S. Baker became a preacher at the First Congregational Church and was ordained in 1883. She also wrote poetry.

25 Captain Charles E. Allen to Lillian Allen, 15 July 1873, Allen Family Papers, Nantucket Historical Association.

26 Ellen B. Dunham to Mrs. James Dunham, 20 December 1870, Collection of William and Ruth Grieder, Nantucket.

27 Coffin School Record Book 4, 1881–1897, Coffin School Papers, Nantucket Historical Association.

28 Ibid.

29 Coffin School Trustees Record Book, 1847–1884, n.p., Coffin School Trustees.

30 George H. Folger to Charles G. Coffin, 30 June 1881, published in Amory, p. 109.

Chapter 4

MANUAL TRAINING & HOME ECONOMICS: 1903–1930S

1 Elizabeth Coffin to Judge Thaddeus Defriez, president of the trustees, 17 June 1902, Edouard A. Stackpole Collection, Nantucket Historical Association.

2 Ibid.

3 The Coffin School Association was disbanded in 1965, when all its funds and scholarships were turned over to the Coffin School Trustees.

4 As early as 1883, the state legalized by statute the then new education.

5 *Inquirer and Mirror,* 10 October 1903.

6 Ibid., 3 December 1904.

7 He was followed by William D. McLemore in 1909, Frank Woodlock in 1911, and Alvin E. Paddock in 1918.

8 *Inquirer and Mirror,* 18 June 1904.

9 There is no solid evidence to support the notion that among the types of baskets made by pupils were the famous Nantucket lightship baskets.

10 *Inquirer and Mirror,* 12 August 1905.

11 *Report Of The Coffin School Association for the Year 1909* (Nantucket, MA: 1909), 3, Nantucket Schools Collection, Nantucket Historical Association.

12 *Statement of the Receipts and Expenditures Of Nantucket Town and County, Together with Reports of the School Committee* (Nantucket, MA: Town of Nantucket, 1908), 83.

13 *The Coffin School Association, Nantucket, Massachusetts, 1910* (Nantucket, MA: 1910), 23, Nantucket Schools Collection, Nantucket Historical Association.

14 The collection of Alfred and Anne Mitchell Macy's books is owned by the Coffin School Trustees, including two books that were a gift to Anne from her sister, Maria Mitchell, the renowned astronomer.

15 She was replaced by Lydia G. Tobey, a dressmaker who had taught sewing for the Golden Rod Club on Nantucket.

16 *Statement of the Receipts and Expenditures of Nantucket Town And County, Together with Reports of the School Committee* (New Bedford, MA: F. S. Brightman Company, 1906), 72.

17 Harriet Barnard (Barrett) Fleming Reminiscences: 1903-1909, Nantucket Historical Association.

18 *Inquirer and Mirror,* 6 January 1906.

19 Other plaster casts remaining in the Coffin School's collection are a "Madonna and Child" relief by Settegnano, two classical busts, and many medallions of the Italian Renaissance period.

20 *Inquirer and Mirror,* 3 December 1904.

21 Ibid., 28 July 1923.

22 Built of brick to match the main building, the new wing cost $9,000.

23 *Twentieth Anniversary of the Coffin School Association* (Nantucket, MA: 1918), n.p., Coffin School Papers, Nantucket Historical Association.

24 Among the assistants who worked in the department were Polly Mayhew and Philice Andrews.

25 *The Coffin School Association, Nantucket, Massachusetts, 1910* (Nantucket, MA: 1910), 24, Nantucket Schools Collection, Nantucket Historical Association.

26 Other teachers who worked in the manual training department were Albert H. Bloomfield and Walter J. Curran.

Chapter 5

Serving the Community: 1940s–Present

1 In order to make the change, the program had to meet state requirements for equipment, the number of hours the boys spent in class, etc. See *Financial Statement of the Town and County of Nantucket, Together With Reports of the School Committee, 1941* (Nantucket, MA: The Inquirer and Mirror Press, 1942), 124-25.

2 *Inquirer and Mirror,* 21 May 1970.